TORNADOES

S E Y M O U R   S I M O N

MORROW JUNIOR BOOKS
New York

PHOTO CREDITS

Permission to use the following photographs is gratefully acknowledged:
front jacket, © David Hoadley 1977; pages 5, 23, Photo Researchers, Inc., © Howard Bluestein;
pages 6–7, National Severe Storms Laboratory/Phil Degginger/Color-Pic, Inc.; pages 12–13,
Joseph H. Bailey, © National Geographic Society; page 15, NWS/Birmingham, AL; page 17,
Chris Johns/National Geographic Image Collection; pages 18–19, NOAA/Corbis; pages 20–21,
E. R. Degginger/Color-Pic, Inc.; page 25, National Center for Atmospheric Research, Boulder,
CO/Harald Richter; pages 26–27, 28, 31, © Jim Reed; page 32, NOAA, National Severe Storms Laboratory;
back jacket, Harald Richter/NOAA, National Severe Storms Laboratory.

Art on page 9 and both maps on page 11 by Ann Neumann.

The text type is 18-point Garamond Book.

Published by Morrow Junior Books
a division of William Morrow and Company, Inc.
1350 Avenue of the Americas, New York, NY 10019
www.williammorrow.com

Printed in Singapore at Tien Wah Press.

1 2 3 4 5 6 7 8 9 10

Library of Congress Cataloging-in-Publication Data
Simon, Seymour.
Tornadoes / Seymour Simon.
p. cm.
Summary: Describes the location, nature, development, measurement, and
destructive effects of tornadoes, as well as how to stay out of danger from them.
ISBN 0-688-14646-5 (trade)—ISBN 0-688-14647-3 (library)
1. Tornadoes—Juvenile literature. [1. Tornadoes.]
I. Title. QC955.2.S56 1999 551.55'3—DC21 98-27953 CIP AC

To Chloe's new brother, Jeremy Scott, with love

Twisters, dust devils, whirlwinds, waterspouts, cyclones—tornadoes go by different names. But whatever they are called, the roaring winds of a tornado can toss a truck high into the air, smash a building, and snap the trunk of a tree like a matchstick.

A tornado's funnel looks like a huge elephant's trunk hanging down from a cloud. The funnel acts like a giant vacuum cleaner—whenever the hose touches the ground, it sucks things up into the air.

Tornadoes (from the Spanish word *tronada,* meaning "thunderstorm") have been reported in every state of the United States and in every season. However, they occur most often in the eastern two-thirds of the country during the spring, which is sometimes called tornado season.

A tornado is a powerfully twisting column of air that makes contact with the ground. It is visible when it contains water droplets in the form of a cloud, or surface dust and debris, or some of both. When a tornado touches down, it usually creates an explosion of dust and wreckage on the ground. If the twisting column of air does not touch down and does not produce damage, it is called a funnel cloud.

Most tornadoes are local storms. A typical tornado

is four hundred to five hundred feet wide, less than a thousand feet long from cloud to ground, and has winds of less than 112 miles per hour. It usually lasts only a few minutes and covers only a few miles on the ground. But a few monster tornadoes are a mile wide and have the strongest winds ever measured in nature: up to 300 miles per hour. They can last for an hour or more and travel more than two hundred miles along the ground, leaving enormous damage in their wake.

The first step in the birth of a tornado is usually a thunderstorm. This type of storm begins when warm, humid air rises upward from the ground. As these updrafts cool in the upper atmosphere, the moisture in them forms clouds. The water droplets or ice crystals in the clouds grow bigger as water vapor around them condenses, or becomes liquid. The droplets or crystals begin to fall, creating downdrafts, and these downdrafts meet new updrafts, which continue feeding warm humid air into the spreading thunderhead cloud.

This is the most violent time in a thunderstorm. A tornado may form at the edge of an updraft, where it meets a downdraft. The updraft pulls air away from the ground, which creates an area of low pressure. More air rushes in to take the place of air that's been pulled up. Then the falling water droplets in the downdraft get swept in and begin to form the tornado's funnel-shaped cloud. As the swirling winds pick up dirt from the ground, the funnel grows darker.

There is a continual battle across North America between large bodies of air called air masses. Air masses can be cool or warm, moist or dry. For example, cool dry air comes from northern lands, while warm moist air comes from the Gulf of Mexico and the Pacific Ocean. Air masses push each other across the lines where they meet, which are called fronts.

As a cool air mass presses forward, it slides underneath a warm air mass and pushes the warm air up. Fast-growing clouds called thunderheads take shape along the front and storms develop. A squall line made up of several thunderstorms may be more than one hundred miles long.

Sometimes a large thunderstorm, called a supercell, forms on the southwestern end of a squall line. Supercells often develop spinning winds inside them called mesocyclones. Some die out after a few minutes, while others spin faster and form funnel clouds at their bases. The strongest tornadoes form in the updraft areas of mesocyclones.

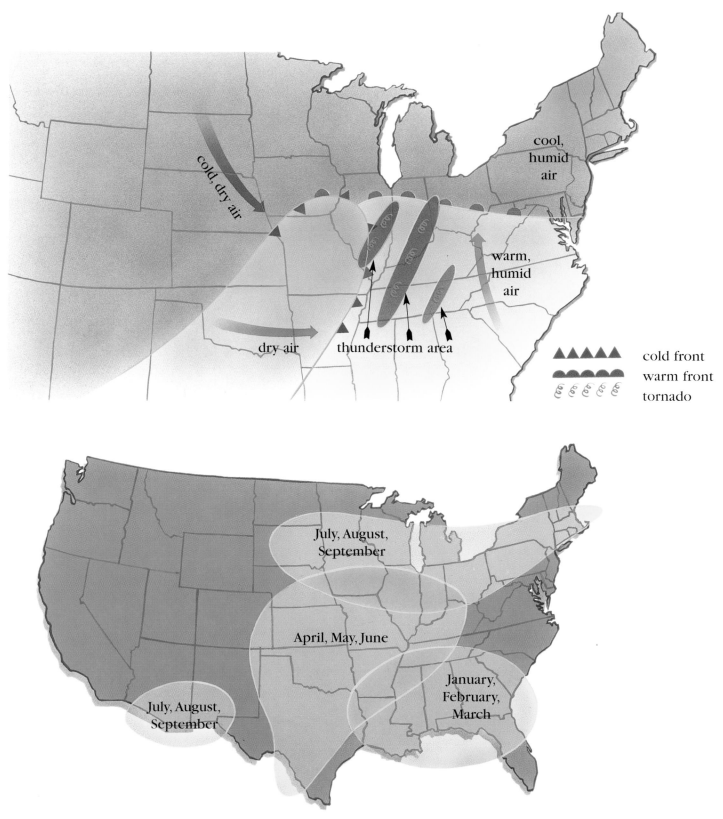

Supercells are most common between April and June. And they are most likely to occur in an area known as tornado alley, which runs from central Texas as far north as Illinois and Indiana and as far east as Kentucky. From January to March, supercells form in some southern states, and from July through September, they can occur in the southwest and the northeast.

Tornadoes born in supercells are hugely powerful. One monster tornado that touched down in Illinois in 1990 lifted a twenty-ton trailer truck from a highway and bounced it up and down like a ball before depositing it in a field eleven hundred feet away. A strong tornado can pick up a house and move it down the block to another lot.

Sometimes tornadoes do odd things. A tornado once sucked up a pond full of frogs and rained them down on a nearby town. Another tornado struck a house and carried a five-hundred-pound piano twelve hundred feet through the air.

One of the worst tornadoes of recent years struck the town of Jarrell, Texas, on May 27, 1997. A thunderstorm came rumbling out of the north in the middle of the afternoon. Moving at a slow 20 miles per hour, the storm entered the town, and several twisters dropped out of the clouds. One resident later said, "That sky was black as night, just boiling."

The largest tornado moved slower and stayed longer; it sat on the ground for fifteen to twenty minutes, destroying everything it touched. The twister sucked trees out of the ground and pulled up nearly a mile of the road leading into town. Driving rain and hail came behind the twister. Survivors opened their eyes to see dark sky where their roofs had been.

By the time the tornado left, fifty homes had been lifted up and smashed down and twenty million dollars of damage had been done to the small town. Twenty-seven people had died, out of a population of one hundred thirty-one.

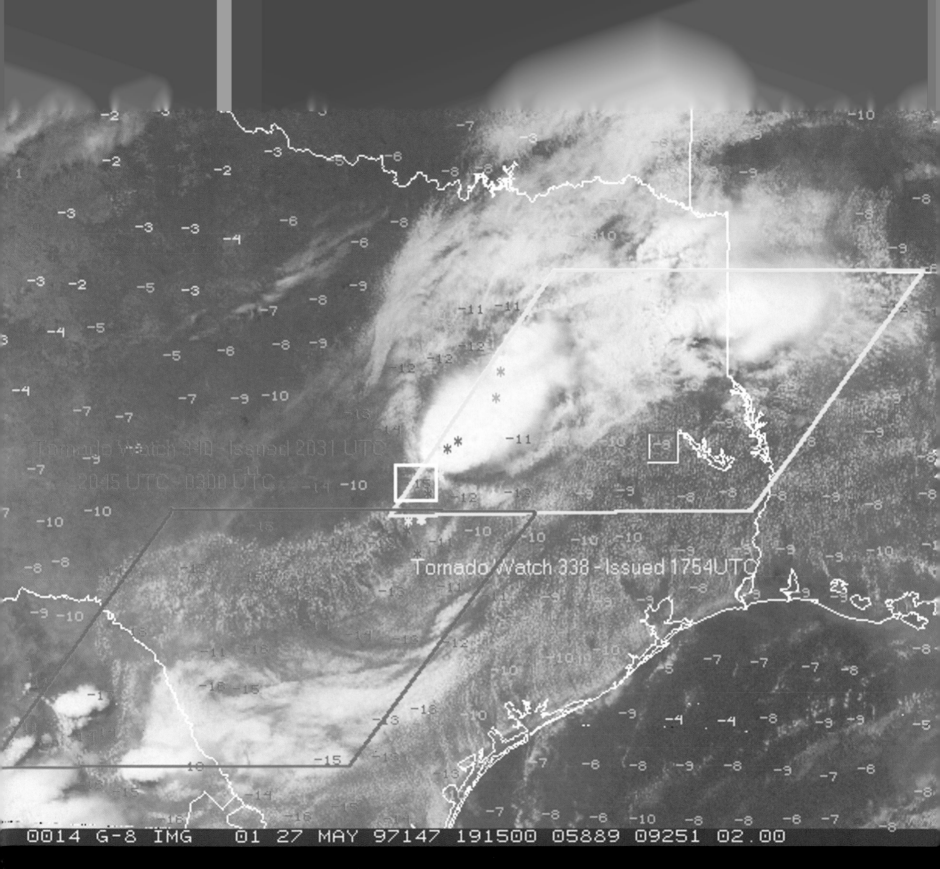

This is a Doppler radar photograph of the area around Jarrell, Texas, on May 27, 1997.
The asterisks show the location of tornado activity. The asterisk in the white box in the
center marks the location of the monster tornado that hit Jarrell.

The single deadliest tornado in history was the Tri-State tornado. It touched down in Missouri on March 18, 1925, in the early afternoon, and swept into Illinois and then Indiana. It sounded like "a thousand freight trains."

The Tri-State tornado traveled along a 219-mile path of death and destruction. In three and a half hours, the tornado killed 689 people, injured 2,000, and left more than 10,000 homeless.

Most tornadoes come singly, but sometimes many travel together. In early April 1998 a line of tornadoes along a thunderstorm ripped through one little town after another in Mississippi, Alabama, and Georgia. The monster tornadoes destroyed hundreds of homes, schools, and churches and caused dozens of deaths. Some people were even sucked out of their homes. Rescue workers compared the destruction to that of a bomb blast.

Fortunately, not all tornadoes are as violent and destructive as the Tri-State tornado of 1925 or the April 1998 tornadoes. Most tornadoes are much weaker.

The Fujita-Pearson Tornado Intensity Scale (or F-Scale) ranks tornadoes according to their wind speed and the kind of damage they can cause. Weak tornadoes are classed as F0 or F1 and are much more common than strong tornadoes. F0 tornadoes have winds that range from 40 to 72 miles per hour. They do light damage to chimneys, TV antennas, and roof shingles. Small tree branches can be broken. Nearly three out of every ten tornadoes are classed as F0.

Slightly greater damage is caused by F1 tornadoes. These storms have winds of 73 to 112 miles per hour. They can uproot some trees, overturn automobiles and small trucks, and push trailers around on the ground. About four out of every ten tornadoes are in the F1 class.

Waterspouts are weak tornadoes that form over warm water. This is a photograph of a waterspout on the ocean. Waterspouts are most common along the Gulf Coast and in the southeastern states.

Strong tornadoes are classed as F2 and F3. F2 tornadoes have winds of between 113 and 157 miles per hour. They cause considerable damage. F2 tornadoes may blow roofs off homes, leaving only strong walls standing. They demolish sheds and small outbuildings. They can overturn mobile homes and cause walls of wooden buildings to collapse. About two to three of every ten tornadoes are classed as F2.

F3 tornadoes cause severe damage, since they have winds ranging from 158 to 206 miles per hour. These tornadoes can flatten all the trees in a forest and collapse metal buildings. They blow off roofs and tumble exterior walls made of concrete blocks. Six out of every hundred tornadoes are classed as F3.

This photograph shows an F3 tornado that hit Marmaduke, Arkansas, in March 1997. It destroyed eleven homes, damaged fifty-seven others, and resulted in one death. The tornado followed a nearly straight line one hundred yards wide and a mile long.

The most violent tornadoes are classed as F4 or F5. An F4 tornado has a wind speed of 207 to 260 miles per hour. Such powerful winds will leave few if any walls standing, even in sturdily built apartment houses. F4 tornadoes can pluck trees up from their roots and break their trunks in half. They can pick up and throw large building materials long distances, hurling them with such force that the materials penetrate concrete. Only two out of every hundred tornadoes are classed as F4.

F5 tornadoes—the highest classification on the F-Scale—are the monster tornadoes. Their winds blow at speeds of more than 261 miles per hour. They can cause incredible damage, including leveling almost any small or medium-sized building and making the land look as if a bulldozer roared across it.

The F5 tornadoes are the rarest. Fewer than one out of every hundred tornadoes is classed as F5. The Tri-State and Jarrell, Texas, tornadoes are examples of how destructive an F5 tornado can be.

Learning about tornadoes can help to save lives. For example, even though the average tornado travels at 30 miles per hour, much faster ground speeds—up to 70 miles per hour—have been reported. That means that trying to flee to safety in an automobile may be reasonable in the country, where the roads are not crowded. But in populated areas, traffic-clogged roads can make it dangerous to get into an automobile.

It is also untrue that tornadoes never strike big cities. For example, Nashville, Tennessee, was badly damaged by a violent tornado in April 1998. And in the past forty years, St. Louis, Missouri, has been hit by tornadoes more than twenty times.

Still another myth is that opening the windows in a house will help prevent it from being destroyed by a tornado. In fact, opening the wrong windows could allow air to rush in and blow the structure apart from inside. The best advice is to forget the windows and get to a shelter.

One of the most important things you can do to prevent injury in a tornado is to be alert to the onset of severe weather. Learn the signs of approaching bad weather, so that you will know to tune in the weather forecasts on TV or radio. If a tornado watch is issued for your area, it means a tornado is possible, because one has already been spotted either on the ground or on radar.

Here are some of the things people hear or see just before a tornado arrives:

- The sky turns a greenish or greenish black color.
- There is a sound a little like rushing air or a waterfall, and it turns into a roar as the tornado comes closer.
- Debris drops from the sky.
- A funnel-shaped cloud appears. It is spinning, while other clouds are moving very quickly toward it.

If a tornado watch or warning is posted, then a real danger sign that a tornado is coming is falling hail.

It is also a good idea to know, *before* a tornado strikes, where to go for shelter. Cars and trailers are *not* safe during a tornado. Go to the basement of a solidly built house. Staying under the stairs or a heavy table helps to protect you from crumbling walls. Blankets can also help to shield you from flying debris.

In an apartment or a home without a basement, an inside room or closet is the safest place. Getting into a bathtub and putting a couch cushion over you helps protect you on all sides. Bathtubs are usually solidly anchored to the ground and sometimes are the only things left in place after a tornado hits.

If you are out walking or biking and are caught in the open when a tornado touches down, lie flat in a ditch or low area if there is *no* rain. If there *is* rain, there may be a danger of flash flooding. Then you should take shelter away from trees and power lines and away from glass windows or doors in houses. Crouch down and make yourself as small a target as possible.

Weather scientists, called meteorologists, are trying to find the best ways to predict and warn against tornadoes. One thing they do is to keep a close watch on severe thunderstorms. They also look for a wall of clouds, which can spawn a tornado. The National Weather Service uses Doppler radar, which can show air movement as well as the shape of clouds. Early signs of rapid air rotation during a thunderstorm can allow life-saving warnings to be issued fifteen to twenty minutes before a tornado forms.

Each year about a thousand tornadoes touch down in the United States, far more than in any other country in the world. Only a small number actually strike occupied buildings, but every year hundreds of people are killed or injured. The chances that a tornado will strike you or a building that you are in are very, very small, though. In fact, you are about as likely to be hit by lightning or to be the victim of a shark attack as to be struck by a tornado.

The best protection from tornadoes comes from receiving an early warning. Listening to local radio or television stations during a weather watch can alert you to take safety measures as soon as a tornado warning is broadcast. You don't have to worry too much in advance about tornadoes, but finding out when they are coming and knowing what to do is certain to help you if one strikes.